Once ι

Wal

ι

Charles Lutwidge Dodgson (1832–1898)
came to Oxford as a Christ Church undergraduate
in 1851, and lived in the city as a student and tutor
for the rest of his life. In 1855, Henry Liddell
(1811–1898) was appointed Dean of the college.
Over the next few years, Dodgson amused himself
by inventing stories, puzzles, and games for the
entertainment of the Dean's young daughters,
Lorina (1849–1930), Edith (1854–1876), and
especially Alice (1852–1934). The result was
the world's most famous children's story, written
under the pseudonym of Lewis Carroll: *Alice's
Adventures in Wonderland* (1865), and its
sequel, *Through the Looking-Glass* (1872).

This booklet describes in two near-circular
walks the locations in Oxford that are relevant to
the creation of the two books, and identifies other
important locations farther afield.

In addition, a short chronology is provided and
brief biographies of some of the individuals who
are thought to have inspired characters such as the
Hatter, the White Rabbit, the Red Queen,
and the Dormouse.

*Please check venue opening times
on the website addresses provided.*

Some Oxford 'characters'

'Lewis CARROLL' (1832–98)

Charles Dodgson chose this pseudonym for his non-academic publications in 1856, by adapting the Latin for his first name of Charles and the anglicised version of his German middle name of Lutwidge. Dodgson was born in Cheshire, the eldest boy and third child in a family of eleven siblings, of whom Frances (1828–1903) and Elizabeth (1830–1916) feature in this guide. He studied at **9** CHRIST CHURCH as an undergraduate from 1851 to 1854. The following year, Henry LIDDELL became Dean of the college, and Dodgson was appointed as a lecturer in mathematics. In *April 1856* came Dodgson's first encounter with Henry Liddell's daughter Alice, the young girl who would inspire the world's most famous children's story. Carroll included himself as the Dodo (an abbreviation of 'Dodgson') in *Wonderland*, and possibly also as the White Knight in *Looking-Glass*. Carroll is buried in Guildford.

Theophilus CARTER (1824–1904)

Carter was an Oxford furniture-maker who is often described as the man upon whom, at Carroll's request, the illustrator of the Alice books, John TENNIEL, based his character of the Hatter. This idea emerged only in the 1930s, in a series of letters written to *The Times* newspaper, where it was also asserted that Carter had invented an alarm-clock bed exhibited at the Great Exhibition in London in 1851. The latter statement is almost certainly untrue, and there is no evidence that Carter had any connection with Tenniel, Carroll, or Alice. It is more likely that he adopted the persona *after* the books had become famous. A more plausible candidate is Thomas RANDALL. Carter's shop **2b** was in the High Street, and he is buried in **13a** HOLYWELL CEMETERY.

Note: *dates in italics* are taken from Lewis Carroll's diaries.

Thomas (1796–1872) & Martha (1806–93) COMBE

Thomas Combe was superintendent of ❶❺ the OXFORD UNIVERSITY PRESS from 1838 until his death in 1872, and oversaw the printing of the first edition of *Wonderland* in July 1865. Combe and his wife Martha befriended and supported many of the Pre-Raphaelite artists whom Lewis Carroll would later photograph. This process commenced in 1850 when the Combes had a chance encounter near Oxford with John Millais (1829–96) and Charles Allston Collins (1828–73). Subsequently Dante Gabriel Rossetti (1828–82), Thomas Woolner (1825–92), and especially William Holman Hunt (1827–1910) benefitted from the Combes' patronage. Most of the Combes' collection of Pre-Raphaelite art was donated to ❶❼ the ASHMOLEAN Museum.

Robinson DUCKWORTH (1834–1911)

A frequent companion on Lewis Carroll's river outings, Duckworth was a Fellow of Trinity College from 1860 to 1876, and tutor to Prince Leopold (Queen Victoria's youngest son). Of the famous voyage to GODSTOW on 4 July 1862, when Alice persuaded Carroll to commit his story of her to paper, Duckworth recalled that 'the story was actually composed and spoken over my shoulder for the benefit of Alice, who was acting as cox'. Duckworth was also present on the *17 June 1862* 'Pool of Tears' trip to SANDFORD, ensuring his immortalisation as the Duck.

Alice LIDDELL (1852–1934)

The real Alice was the daughter of the Dean of ❾ CHRIST CHURCH, Henry Liddell (1811–98), who is sometimes thought to have been the inspiration for the White Rabbit, as his multiple responsibilities meant that he was often late for meetings and appointments. He and his wife (née Lorina Reeve, 1826–1910) moved to Oxford in 1855 from London, where Alice was born on 4 May 1852. She was nearly four when Lewis Carroll first made her acquaintance, and was ten on 4 July 1862, the day of the fateful river outing to GODSTOW, although Carroll contrived her fictional self to be seven in the books, in which her two sisters Lorina (1849–1930) and Edith (1854–76) both also feature. Alice married a Christ Church graduate, Reginald Hargreaves, in 1880. The couple had three boys, two of whom died in the First World War. She is buried at Lyndhurst, in Hampshire, where she lived for most of her married life.

Mary PRICKETT (1832–1920)

Mary Prickett found employment as governess to the LIDDELL family soon after their arrival in Oxford in 1855, and continued in this role until shortly before her marriage in 1870. She first came to Lewis Carroll's attention on *3 November 1856*, when she was out walking with Lorina Liddell, and she was inevitably almost always present on the many other occasions when Carroll met the children or took walks with them. She sometimes went on boat outings too. There seems little doubt that it was Mary whom Carroll had in mind as the model for the Red Queen in *Through the Looking-Glass*: 'the concentrated essence of all governesses', as he called the character some years later. She was born in Oxford (not BINSEY, as suggested in many publications), and after her marriage she ran the prestigious ❶ MITRE INN for almost 50 years.

Thomas Jones PROUT (1823–1909)

Lewis Carroll's lifelong friend Thomas Prout held the living of St Margaret's Church at BINSEY from 1857 until 1891. Prout had a reputation for dozing off during the sometimes tedious staff meetings held at ❾ CHRIST CHURCH, so in view of his direct association with the church's Treacle Well – it was Prout who arranged for the restoration of the well in 1874 and erected the tablet which records its legendary significance – he is an especially good candidate for the original of the Dormouse.

Thomas RANDALL (1805–87)

Although in 1932 Alice remembered Thomas Randall of ❼ GRANDPONT HOUSE as 'a well-known Oxford tailor', he himself preferred to be known as a 'hatter'.

A well-known local character, he was called 'jolly Tom Randall' by one contemporary, and 'the link between the town and the gown' (i.e. between those age-old foes, the inhabitants and tradesmen of Oxford on the one hand and the University on the other). He became Mayor of Oxford in 1859, and had many connections with ⑨ CHRIST CHURCH. Among these was the friendship of his daughter Eliza (1836–1916) with Mary PRICKETT and with the LIDDELL family, and Eliza's marriage to the Christ Church graduate and eminent musician (Sir) John Stainer (1840–1901). Randall and the Stainers are buried at ⑬ₐ HOLYWELL.

John RUSKIN (1819–1900)

John Ruskin studied at ⑨ CHRIST CHURCH between 1837 and 1839, becoming acquainted then with Henry LIDDELL, also a Christ Church graduate and then tutor. Ruskin became the leading English art critic of the Victorian era, and returned to Oxford in 1870 to take up a post as Professor of Fine Art. Ruskin had remained friendly with Liddell, and provided instruction for his daughters. It is therefore Ruskin who springs to mind when the Mock Turtle says, 'The Drawling-master was an old conger-eel that used to come once a week: *he* taught us Drawling, Stretching, and Fainting in Coils' (i.e. drawing, sketching, and painting in oils).

Sir John TENNIEL (1820–1914)

When Lewis Carroll persuaded so eminent a figure as John Tenniel to illustrate *Alice's Adventures in Wonderland*, it was undoubtedly a very shrewd move. Tenniel was the principal illustrator of the highly popular *Punch* magazine, and Carroll of course was at that time totally unknown. The instant success of *Alice's Adventures* probably had much to do with the pictures, as Carroll himself acknowledged. They ensured not only that its appeal, and that of *Looking-Glass*, would endure for over 150 years, but also that Tenniel's fame would remain far greater through them than for the many hundreds of his drawings in *Punch*.

Mary Prickett (1832–1920)

Alice with the Red Queen in 'The Garden of Live Flowers'
(*Looking-Glass*)

Alice in Waterland

Three waterways, boats and barges, water meadows, the ox and the ford, and Oxford's most river-oriented college.

Distance from the Visitor Information Centre in Broad Street to the final location: approximately 2 miles.

 From Broad Street, turn right into Turl Street. On the left is Exeter College, where Oxford author Philip Pullman was a student. Parts of his fantasy trilogy *His Dark Materials* are set in an imaginary Oxford, where Exeter College has been replaced by Jordan College, the home of his own Alice-equivalent young heroine, Lyra. *Northern Lights*, the first part, was adapted for film as 'The Golden Compass', for which the rooftop architecture of Exeter College was reproduced in the studio. At the end of Turl Street is the Mitre Inn, best viewed from the opposite side of the High Street. Cross at the lights, then turn left to walk away from the city centre.

① MITRE INN 18 High Street

www.beefeatergrill.co.uk/beefeater/restaurants/oxford/the-mitre.html

There are records of an inn at this location since the 13th century, though the present building dates from about 1630. By the 19th century it had become one of the city's principal coaching inns, ideally placed for regular services to and from London and elsewhere. The LIDDELL family's governess, Mary PRICKETT, and her new husband, Charles Foster, took over as proprietors in 1870, after Mary had left the family's service. She continued to run the inn alone after the death of her husband in 1888 until her own death in 1920. It is possible that one landlord in the 14th century had a longer tenure, but otherwise hers, of nearly 50 years, is the longest known.

Note: *Dates in italics* indicate information taken from Lewis Carroll's diaries.

Thomas Randall (1805–1887)

The 'Mad Tea-Party' (*Wonderland*)

② 22 HIGH STREET

The fourth shop down from All Saints' Church (at the corner of Turl Street and High Street) is where the tailor, hosier, and hatter Thomas RANDALL was in business from at least 1825 until 1864. Well known to the LIDDELL family, he is a recent candidate as the inspiration for the character of the Hatter.

EITHER proceed down the narrow alley called Oriel Street, noting NO. 6 on the right, which displays both the city arms (the ox and ford) and the arms of the Bishop of Oxford (the ox and three princesses). Through Canterbury Gate, the exit from ⑨ CHRIST CHURCH at the corner of Oriel Square, the end of the college's Library is visible. This is where Lewis Carroll once had an office overlooking the Dean's garden. Walk away from this gate along Merton Street as far as the large metal gates on the right and follow the path between Corpus Christi and Merton Colleges.

On entering Merton Field through a very narrow gate (which is locked at dusk), turn left along the path known as 'Deadman's Walk', keeping the old city wall and Merton College to your left. (Near the end note the memorial on the wall to a pioneer of hot-air ballooning, the Oxford pastry-cook James Sadler.) At the end of the path beyond the railings you will see ③ the BOTANIC GARDENS.

OR continue down the High (eastwards).

②a OLD BANK & QUOD 92–94 High Street

www.quod.co.uk

The hotel and restaurant called the Old Bank is where Carroll's own bank of Parsons Thompson once traded. He banked there from its opening in 1856 until his account was closed by his executors in 1900. His bank statements show that he generously supported his unmarried sisters and younger brothers after the death of their father in 1868. He also made numerous regular charitable donations, most notably to organisations helping disadvantaged women and children. Presumably the payment of £5 that he made on 5 August 1873, credited merely to 'Hatter', was not a charitable one, however – even if the character does state twice (at the trial of the Knave of Hearts) that 'I'm a poor man'! Later taken over by Barclays, the building was converted into a hotel in 1999.

Theophilus Carter
(1824–1904),
taken c.1900

The Botanic Gardens and Magdalen Tower,
seen from the Cherwell

2b 48 & 49 HIGH STREET

On the north side of the High, just before Longwall Street, are the premises once occupied by Theophilus CARTER, who is often stated to be the man who inspired John TENNIEL's depiction of the Hatter. (Although this is actually very unlikely, the premises at No. 48 did have a later connection with a genuinely important Oxford individual, the car-manufacturer William Morris, later Lord Nuffield, who repaired and manufactured cycles and motor-bicycles here from 1896 to 1908.) Carter traded mainly as a furniture maker from one, sometimes both, of the two properties from at least 1861 until 1894, and from other premises just off the High Street for at least ten years prior to that.

 The entrance to the oldest botanic gardens in Britain (1621) is from the High Street, opposite Magdalen College, but the grounds can also be seen by entering ④ CHRIST CHURCH MEADOW through the narrow gate at the end of Rose Lane, past Deadman's Walk on the right, and walking straight on towards the River ⑤ CHERWELL.

3 BOTANIC GARDEN

www.botanic-garden.ox.ac.uk

On 30 June 1860 a celebration was held here after a famous British Association debate on evolution at the newly opened University Museum (see ⑭ MUSEUM OF NATURAL HISTORY). This was the year after the publication of Charles Darwin's *On the Origin of Species*, and the party was organised to celebrate the perceived success of those who espoused the Darwinian theory. (Note the ape in both illustrations on page 32.) In the days that followed, Lewis Carroll photographed a number of the important individuals who were present in Oxford at the time.

The Garden also features in Oxford author Philip Pullman's fantasy trilogy, *His Dark Materials*, as the setting for the last chapter of the third book, *The Amber Spyglass*.

'A Punting Scene' *c.*1850 (Edward Bradley)

'The Queen's Croquet-Ground' (*Wonderland*)

4 CHRIST CHURCH MEADOW

We know from Lewis Carroll's diaries that he often walked around the low-lying, marshy land which is bordered by the Rivers CHERWELL and THAMES (to the east and south), the TRILL MILL STREAM (to the west), and the Broad Walk (to the north). Often he met Alice and her sisters on these walks, accompanied by their governess, Mary PRICKETT. In essence, the path, the rivers, and the appearance of the tree-fringed meadow will not have changed very much since those days, and in the right conditions the Meadow can present a beguiling sense of timelessness. In summer you can see English Longhorn Cattle on the Meadow.

5 RIVER CHERWELL

Although Carroll often took the LIDDELL sisters for boat trips on the River Thames, he made few references to the Cherwell in his diaries. However, one significant event on its banks was recorded there on *10 March 1863*, the day when Albert the Prince of Wales (later King Edward VII) married Princess Alexandra of Denmark. While walking around CHRIST CHURCH MEADOW that day, Carroll stopped to watch '*the three Deanery children plant three trees along the Cherwell, in memory of the day*'. Each of the girls, Lorina, Alice, and Edith, '*delivered a short speech over her tree "long life to this tree, and may it prosper from this auspicious day," and they named them Alexandra, Albert, and Victoria*' (the latter being the Prince's mother, Queen Victoria). In June 1863, the Prince and Princess stayed at CHRIST CHURCH (where Edward had been an undergraduate) and on the afternoon of *17 June* they found time to play croquet with the Liddell girls. Croquet was a game the girls enjoyed playing with Carroll too, on *3 July* and *2 August 1862*, for instance.

As you walk with the river to your left, two branches unite about 150 yards beyond the Broad Walk. About 200 yards farther the river divides again. The left-hand branch is known as the New Cut, having been created in 1884 to divert water away from the Meadow at times of flood; the path follows the Cherwell's more natural course as it meanders to the right. The

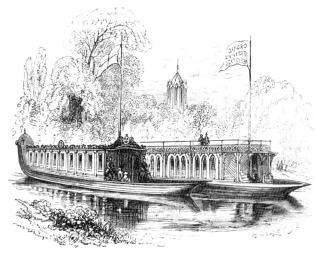

College Barges *c*.1859 (from *The Book of the Thames*, 1859)

Oxford's Eight, 1872

views back across the Meadow on this section of the walk are as evocative as any in Oxford of the poet Matthew Arnold's famous 'city of dreaming spires'. At the confluence with the River Thames, the villages of IFFLEY, SANDFORD, and Nuneham (a favourite destination) are to your left, about one, two and a half, and five miles downstream respectively.

RIVER THAMES

In the mid-19th century the bank of CHRIST CHURCH MEADOW was lined with ornate college barges. These were introduced as changing rooms for the oarsmen involved in the regular rowing competitions which are still held on this stretch of the river and also as viewing platforms for spectators. Lewis Carroll's first ever diary reference to Dean LIDDELL's family came while watching some boat races here, on *25 February 1856*, when he first met Mrs Liddell and her *'two eldest children'* (i.e. Harry, the oldest, who was born in 1847, and Lorina).

👈 Stop at the junction of the avenue which leads directly towards CHRIST CHURCH, sometimes called the Long Walk. On the opposite bank of the Thames, behind a prominent footbridge, is Grandpont House.

GRANDPONT HOUSE

As a child, Alice was a frequent visitor to the three-storey Georgian mansion (built in 1785) which is set back from the main Thames on the southern bank opposite. She later described it as 'a house built on arches over the Isis*', a description which is expanded in the 1850's novel *The Adventures of Mr. Verdant Green* as 'that eccentric mansion' which 'instead of cellars, appears to have an ingenious system of small rivers to thoroughly irrigate its foundations'. This was the home of a well-known Oxford tailor and hatter, Thomas RANDALL (formerly living at ② 22 HIGH STREET). Alice remembered that a 'special pleasure'

---

* 'Isis' is a former alternative name for the 'Thames', applied to the river only in and near Oxford.

Grandpont House

College boat houses at the confluence of
the Thames and Cherwell

was to be allowed to take his retriever dog Rover out for walks. The unpublished diary of Randall's daughter Eliza shows that Alice and her sisters visited the House often in the early 1860s, with their governess, Mary PRICKETT, whom Eliza counted as a friend. Eliza used to refer to the LIDDELL girls collectively as Mary's 'chicks'.

The name Grandpont derives from the original Norman bridge across the Thames here. The bridge, which probably marks the location of the original ford which gave the city of Oxford its name, is now popularly called Folly Bridge. The part of Oxford to the south of the bridge is still known as Grandpont.

8   TRILL MILL STREAM

If you continue to the end of the riverside path you will reach the confluence of the Trill Mill Stream and the Thames. This is probably where Carroll hired rowing boats to take the children out on the river. Certainly, this is what Alice's son, Caryl Hargreaves, believed. Writing in 1932, he asked his readers to imagine Carroll and Robinson DUCKWORTH escorting the three LIDDELL girls from CHRIST CHURCH 'down to Salter's, where the rowing boats are kept, and watch them choose a nice roomy boat, and plenty of comfortable cushions'. Salter Brothers have built and hired boats here since 1858, and, still owned by the same family, the company continues to hire out small boats and punts to the present day. There is also a summer passenger service to Abingdon via IFFLEY, SANDFORD, and past Nuneham (www.salterssteamers.co.uk).

The river outings were fundamental to the creation of *Alice's Adventures* for three main reasons. Often they would last a whole day, giving Carroll ample opportunity – perhaps even an obligation – to keep his young passengers amused by inventing his tales; some scenes within the stories are clearly based on their actual experiences on the river; and it is likely that riverside places, people, and events inspired some of the characters and episodes. In addition, it was on a river trip to GODSTOW, on 4 July 1862, that the

Folly Bridge from the west

Alice, Lorina, Harry, and Edith Liddell, 1860,
taken by Charles Dodgson

concept of 'Alice' was born, when Carroll undertook to write down the stories. A more detailed account is in *Alice in Waterland* (see inside back cover). A variety of river excursions – some on the theme of 'Alice', with optional commentary – are offered by Oxford River Cruises, based at The Folly riverside restaurant (www.oxfordrivercruises.com).

 The offices of both boat companies (and a footbridge from which to view GRANDPONT HOUSE) can be reached by walking across Folly Bridge after passing through a narrow gate and across a footbridge over the Trill Mill Stream. You will pass The Head of the River public house, which was formerly a Salters' warehouse, built in 1835/36. 'Head of the River' is the term applied to the winning boat of the annual inter-college Eights' Week races, which are held just downstream each summer.

To continue on the main route, take the Long Walk, the tree-lined avenue which leads directly towards Christ Church. It was created on the instructions of Henry LIDDELL in 1872, as a more direct and attractive route to and from the stately college barges than walking alongside the formerly polluted Trill Mill Stream.

9 CHRIST CHURCH

www.chch.ox.ac.uk

Christ Church is the college where Charles Dodgson ('Lewis Carroll') was an undergraduate from 1851 to 1854, acquiring a first-class degree in mathematics and a third in classics. He retained lodgings within the college for the rest of his life. In 1855, Henry LIDDELL was appointed Dean of the college, and over the next few years the friendship which would result in the world's most famous children's story developed between Carroll and the Dean's young daughters: Lorina, Edith, and especially Alice.

The entrance to the college is through the Meadow Building, near where the Long Walk meets the Broad Walk. In brief, from inside the college, you can see: the outside of Lewis Carroll's rooms, where he also had a photographic darkroom; the entrance to the Library (where he once had an office, overlooking the Dean's private garden); and the front of the Deanery, where

CHRIST CHURCH

Emery Walker after E. H. New 1916

1 Canterbury Gate
2 Library
3 Deanery Garden
4 Deanery
5 Cathedral
6 Meadow Building
7 Great Hall
8 Tom Tower
9 Carroll's rooms 1868–1898

Image courtesy of Sanders of Oxford, 104 High Street, Oxford

20

Alice's family once lived. The Cathedral contains the shrine of Oxford's patron saint, St Frideswide, supposed founder of the Treacle Well at BINSEY. There is also a stained-glass window in which Alice's sister Edith (who died suddenly at the age of 22) is depicted as St Catherine. It was while taking photographs of the Cathedral on *25 April 1856* that Carroll first made the acquaintance of Alice.

Above the entrance to the Great Hall (nowadays renowned as the original of Hogwarts Hall, as seen in the films of J. K. Rowling's 'Harry Potter') is a painting of Henry Liddell, and a portrait of Lewis Carroll hangs immediately to your right on entering. High up on the left-hand side, one of the large multi-paned windows contains images of Alice, of Carroll, and of many Wonderland characters. Beneath that window is a fireplace with two brass firedogs with elongated necks, a possible influence for the 'immense length of neck, which seemed to rise like a stalk' that Alice grows after nibbling a piece of the Caterpillar's mushroom.

Within the Deanery Garden (not normally accessible to the public, except on guided tours) is a very old horse-chestnut tree, often identified (more in hope than conviction!) as the one where the Cheshire Cat first appears to Alice. The character was not invented by Carroll – the expression 'to grin like a Cheshire Cat' was already in common parlance – but it represents a small autobiographical reference, Carroll having been born in Cheshire.

 ALICE'S SHOP 83 St Aldate's

www.aliceinwonderlandshop.co.uk

Almost immediately opposite the main exit from CHRIST CHURCH MEADOW is 'Alice's Shop', which sells Alice memorabilia of every conceivable kind. It was first identified as the shop depicted in Tenniel's illustrations for 'Wool & Water' (*Through the Looking-Glass*) in the 1920s, when it was described in a periodical as 'that "little dark shop" ... the only shop in St. Aldates that has retained its original small-paned windows and the counter as shown in the pictures'. It was first given the name 'Alice's Shop' in the 1950s.

'Wool and Water' (*Looking-Glass*)

Alice's Shop, *c.*1950

In J. C. Masterman's 1952 novel *To Teach the Senators Wisdom*, one of the characters calls it 'the authentic sweet shop which Alice visited in *Through the Looking-glass*'.

In Alice's day, the proprietors were John and Mary Millin, and it seems reasonable to assume that to Alice's young eyes Mary either resembled or had a voice like a Sheep. The transformation in 'Wool & Water' from the Shop to a rowing boat seems likely to have been influenced by the frequency with which the locality was affected by floods before the New Cut was made on the ⑤ CHERWELL in 1884. The shop is below street level, and must have been very vulnerable to flooding, which was especially severe in 1852 and 1860. The images in the book are the reverse of reality, in that the door is on the 'wrong' side – but this reversal is of course perfectly compatible with the 'Looking-Glass world' that Alice has entered.

 Walk up St Aldate's towards the city centre, noting the non-public entrance to CHRIST CHURCH beneath Tom Tower (built by Christopher Wren, 1681–2) and the rooms in which Lewis Carroll resided from October 1868 until his death, on the first floor of the double bastion which comprises the left-hand corner.

⑪ STORY MUSEUM   Rochester House, Pembroke Street

www.storymuseum.org.uk

The Story Museum celebrates stories in all forms and explores their enduring power to teach and delight. Since 2007 it has coordinated Alice's Day, with a wide range of themed events, activities, and exhibitions across Oxford on the first Saturday of July (commemorating the *4 July 1862* boat trip to GODSTOW). The Story Museum is working (2016) to create a world centre of children's literature and storytelling in the heart of Oxford. It offers a varied programme of events, talks, and workshops for all ages 'as the fairy dust starts to transform its dilapidated and eccentric home'. The venue has a shop, café, and other new facilities.

MUSEUM OF OXFORD Town Hall, St Aldate's

www.oxford.gov.uk/museumofoxford

This small museum packs many centuries of Oxford's past into a small space. Of note are some of Alice LIDDELL's and Lewis Carroll's personal possessions, and various items of memorabilia, including toffee tins, playing cards, and chess pieces inspired by the stories. Visitors can also take a virtual bike ride from the city and along sections of the River Thames to IFFLEY via CHRIST CHURCH, ALICE'S SHOP, and Folly Bridge.

There are regular drop-in amusements for families, from gallery trails, costumes, and simple art and craft activities to family fun days in the school holidays. There are public conveniences at the Town Hall, and a gift shop.

Christ Church

Some important dates

27 Jan. 1832	Charles Lutwidge Dodgson born.
Jan. 1851–1854	Dodgson an undergraduate at Christ Church, studying classics and mathematics.
4 May 1852	Alice Pleasance Liddell (1852–1934) born. Her relevant siblings were 'Harry' (1847–1911), Lorina Charlotte (1849–1930), Edith (1854–1876), and Rhoda (1859–1949).
June 1855	Henry Liddell appointed Dean of Christ Church.
March 1856	'Lewis Carroll' first adopted as Charles Dodgson's penname.
25 April 1856	Dodgson's first encounter with Alice.
Dec. 1861	Dodgson ordained by the Bishop of Oxford.
4 July 1862	The boat trip to Godstow, acknowledged as the day when the story of Alice was created.
Nov. 1864	Manuscript of 'Alice's Adventures under Ground' completed.
4 July 1865	*Alice's Adventures in Wonderland* printed, recalled, and republished later that year.
Dec. 1871	*Through the Looking-Glass* published (dated 1872).
Sept. 1880	Alice Liddell married Reginald Hargreaves.
14 Jan. 1898	Death of Charles Dodgson
16 Nov. 1934	Death of Alice Hargreaves (née Liddell)

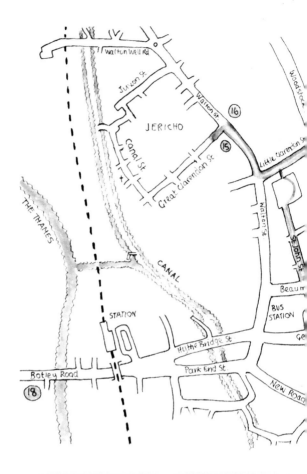

1   MITRE INN

2   22 HIGH STREET

2a   OLD BANK AND QUOD

2b   48 & 49 HIGH STREET

3   BOTANIC GARDENS

4   CHRIST CHURCH MEADOW

5   RIVER CHERWELL

6   RIVER THAMES

7   GRANDPONT HOUSE

8   TRILL MILL STREAM

9   CHRIST CHURCH

10   ALICE'S SHOP

11   STORY MUSEUM

12   MUSEUM OF OXFORD

13   MUSEUM OF THE HISTORY OF SCIENCE

13a   HOLYWELL CEMETERY

14   MUSEUM OF NATURAL HISTORY

15   OXFORD UNIVERSITY PRESS (OUP)

16   ST PAUL'S CHURCH (FREUD'S)

17   ASHMOLEAN MUSEUM

18   ST FRIDESWIDE'S CHURCH, OSNEY

Approximate scale:

200 metres

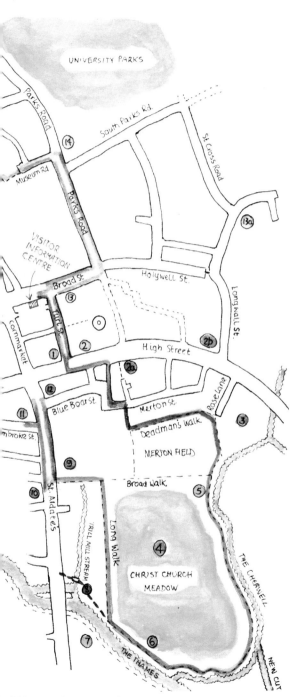

University Parks

Parks Road

South Parks Rd.

St Cross Road

Museum Rd.

Parks Road

⑭

Visitor Information Centre

Broad St.

⑬

Holywell St.

Longwall St.

⑬a

Turl St.

Cornmarket

①

②

◯

High Street

⑫

⑪

Blue Boar St.

Pembroke St.

2a

Merton St.

Rose Lane

2b

Deadman's Walk

③

MERTON FIELD

⑨

Broad Walk

⑩

St. Aldates

⑤

TRILL MILL STREAM

Long Walk

④

CHRIST CHURCH MEADOW

⑧

THE CHERWELL

⑦

⑥

THE THAMES

NEW CUT

The Lewis Carroll Society

The LCS was formed in 1969 to promote interest in the life and works of Charles Lutwidge Dodgson.

The Society has members around the world, including leading libraries, authors, researchers and many who simply enjoy Carroll's books and want to find out more about the author and his work. We have an exciting programme of talks, tours, conferences and other events and we publish regular newsletters and journals offering something for all tastes.

Why not join us?
Our subscription rates are remarkably low.
Full details at:
www.lewiscarrollsociety.org.uk

OXFORD RIVER CRUISES

Our sightseeing river tours, boat trips and private hire cruises take in the stunning scenery of the River Thames in and around Oxford.

Cruises vary from a short trip along the famous University Regatta rowing course alongside Christ Church Meadow, and onwards towards Sandford – scene of 'The Pool of Tears' – to the extraordinary upstream expanse of Port Meadow, following the route of the most famous of all of the real Alice's river journeys with Lewis Carroll in July 1862.

Mad Hatter's Tea Parties and expert commentary by the author of 'Alice's Oxford on Foot' also available.

BOATS DEPART FROM:
No. 1 Folly Bridge
St Aldate's
Oxford OX1 4JU
www.oxfordrivercruises.com
tel: 0845 2269396

Alice in Wanderland

Museums of science, nature, and culture; two streets of diverse shops, cafés, and restaurants; University Parks; and the maze-like suburb of Jericho.

Distance from the Visitor Information Centre in Broad Street to the final location: approximately 1½ miles, or 2 miles with detour.

13 MUSEUM OF THE HISTORY OF SCIENCE Broad Street

www.mhs.ox.ac.uk   Closed Mondays and most mornings

Here you can see the portable case of chemicals that Lewis Carroll used to sensitise the glass plates required in the wet collodian photographic process, as well as an example of the sort of early camera he would have used. Carroll first acquired a camera in *May 1856*, and it was while helping a friend to take photographs within CHRIST CHURCH on *25 April 1856* that he first met Alice. Subsequently he took numerous photographs of Alice and her sisters, as well as of a large number of friends and acquaintances. Of note, these included the Pre-Raphaelite artists William Holman Hunt, John Millais, and Dante Gabriel Rossetti, all of whom benefitted from the patronage of Thomas COMBE.

To reach 14 the MUSEUM OF NATURAL HISTORY:

EITHER (if a longer route is desired: allow at least an extra 30 minutes) walk to the end of Holywell Street and turn left into St Cross Road,

OR walk up Parks Road, noting on the left the gateway to Trinity College, where Robinson DUCKWORTH was a Fellow.

Note: *Dates in italics* indicate information taken from Lewis Carroll's diaries.

The gravestone of Thomas Randall and family,
and beyond it that of John Stainer and family

The gravestone of Theophilus Carter (foreground)

Enter the Cemetery, a haven of urban nature conservation, through the wooden gates, not the metal ones which lead to the church. This is where Thomas RANDALL and Theophilus CARTER – both linked with the character of the Hatter – are buried. Their graves can be located by consulting the plan near the bench by the main central path. The grave of Sir John Stainer, Randall's son-in-law, is No. 21 on the plan (buried with his wife, Randall's daughter, Eliza, beneath a tall stone cross). Randall's own grave, with a slightly smaller cross, is only a few feet away.

Theophilus Carter's gravestone is much eroded, but if you follow the path which leads directly from St Cross Church, and go straight on where it is crossed by another path which leads to the grave of the 'Inkling' writer Charles Williams (No. 34) on the left, it is on the immediate right of the path, almost opposite a grey granite obelisk. The inscriptions on the adjacent graves of other members of Carter's family are more clearly legible.

Also buried here, close to the entrance gate, on the left-hand side of the path as you leave (No. 20), is Kenneth Grahame (1859–1932), the author of *The Wind in the Willows*. He attended school in Oxford, and his inscription reads: 'passed the river on the 6th of July 1932, leaving childhood and literature through him the more blest for all time'. His son Alastair, for whom the story was created, is buried with him, having died aged 20 while a ⑨ CHRIST CHURCH undergraduate.

Continue northwards along St Cross Road. Where it turns sharply left, to become South Parks Road, enter University Parks, another splendid place in which simply to wander! Bear right to find the River CHERWELL or, to continue on the shortest route, bear left, keeping the University buildings to your left. In 1867, when it was proposed to use part of the park for the University cricket pitch, Carroll circulated a poem, 'The Deserted Park', which helped to stop the plan, albeit only temporarily. It contains the lines:

> *Amidst thy bowers the tyrant's hand is seen,*
> *And rude pavilions sadden all your green;*
> *One selfish pastime grasps the whole domain;*
> *And half a faction swallows up the plain.*
> *Adown thy glades, all sacrificed to cricket,*
> *The hollow-sounding bat now guards the wicket.*

'The Pool of Tears' from *The Nursery Alice*, 1889, (above)
and as illustrated by Charles Dodgson
in 'Alice's Adventures under Ground' (below).
See SANDFORD-ON-THAMES.

On leaving University Parks, turn left into Parks Road, with Keble College (founded 1868) on your right. Be alert for bicycles!

14 MUSEUM OF NATURAL HISTORY Parks Road

www.oum.ox.ac.uk

The Museum contains the head and foot of a dodo, the most complete soft-tissue remains anywhere of the extinct bird which Carroll incorporated into the episode of 'The Pool of Tears' as a self-mocking representation of himself. Because of his slight stutter, 'Do-do-Dodgson' is perhaps how he sometimes pronounced his real name. Who knows, possibly the idea of including the bird as a Wonderland character occurred to him when he visited the Museum with Alice, Edith, and Mary PRICKETT on *24 February 1863*. The Museum also possesses a 1651 painting of a dodo; it was extinct by 1680.

The Museum opened in 1860, and almost immediately, on 30 June, hosted a famous debate on Charles Darwin's controversial theory of evolution. The speakers were the botanist Thomas Huxley and the Bishop of Oxford, Samuel Wilberforce. Carroll almost certainly attended the debate, the payment of two guineas that he made to the British Association on 25 June being presumably a subscription made expressly to qualify for admittance to an event which was so eagerly anticipated that as many as one thousand people are thought to have squeezed in to hear it. The debate acquired particular notoriety and significance because of one unwise retort made by Wilberforce in reference to the descent of Huxley's grandparents from apes.

Carroll photographed Wilberforce prior to the debate, and later that week also took pictures of many other famous people who had come to Oxford for the occasion. These included the Pre-Raphaelite artists William Holman Hunt and Thomas Woolner, and the architect of the new Museum, Benjamin Woodward. See also ③ the BOTANIC GARDENS.

The Eagle & Child public house, St Giles

The inclusion of an ape or monkey in the illustration of 'The Pool of Tears' is therefore probably not mere whim. Carroll included one among the 'curious creatures' depicted in the original version of this episode in the handwritten, self-illustrated manuscript he called 'Alice's Adventures under Ground' (see GODSTOW and SANDFORD). John TENNIEL followed suit in *Wonderland*. It is a topical reference to the continuing intellectual argument. There is a statue of Darwin towards the back of the Museum, and nearby are two carved monkeys, one covering its eyes, one its mouth. Alice might well have seen Wonderland creatures such as a turtle, flamingo, hedgehog, and eagle when visiting the Museum. Nowadays you can also see a white rabbit (complete with watch!).

The design of the building, which was opposed by conservative elements within the University, owes much to the influence of the writer and art critic John RUSKIN. Carroll liked the building, praising it in 'The Deserted Park' (1867) as:

> *Museum! Loveliest building of the plain*
> *Where Cherwell winds towards the distant main;*
> *How often have I loitered o'er your green,*
> *Where humble happiness endeared the scene!*

☞ Cross Parks Road at the lights to reach Museum Road. Where it turns abruptly right to become Blackhall Road, walk straight on through Lamb & Flag Passage to the wide thoroughfare of St Giles'. Immediately opposite is The Eagle and Child public house (known locally as 'The Bird and Babe') where C. S. Lewis, J. R. R. Tolkien, and other writers (including Charles Williams – see ⓭ⓐ HOLYWELL) used to meet from the 1930s to the 1960s under the collective name of The Inklings. Turn right to cross Banbury Road at the lights, take the path alongside St Giles' Church, cross Woodstock Road at the lights, and walk down Little Clarendon Street, with its range of small shops, cafés, and restaurants. At the end, turn right into Walton Street (exactly as Philip Pullman's Lyra did in *Lyra's Oxford*).

◀ Oxford University Press, c.1850,
seen from the Oxford Canal
(detail from a view by Carl Rundt)

Thomas Combe (1796–1872)

Martha Combe (née Edwards, 1806–1893)

http://www.oup.com/uk/archives

The University decided to move its Press from the city centre in 1827, and by 1832 the new building in Jericho was fully functioning, on the edge of what had formerly been open fields to the north. This is where 2,000 copies of the first edition of *Alice's Adventures in Wonderland* were printed in July 1865 – although because the illustrator John TENNIEL was dissatisfied with the quality of the printing, this edition was never distributed. Carroll had already dispatched 50 special presentation copies, however, of which 23 are known to have survived. The ledger detailing the considerable cost of £142 19s 2d, which Carroll paid himself, is on display in the OUP museum, which can only be visited by prior appointment (tel: 01865 353527). The rejected pages were subsequently rebound for an American edition of 1866, a copy of which is also on display, as well as the specialised stereotype plate used to print the intricate Mouse's 'Long Tale' page in *Wonderland*.

Thomas COMBE was the superintendent of the Press at this time, living with his wife Martha in a large house overlooking the interior quadrangle. It was in their house on *19 October 1863* that Carroll met Alexander Macmillan, who subsequently agreed to publish the book. The Combes were great patrons of the arts, and are especially important for championing the works of the Pre-Raphaelite Brotherhood. It was through the Combes that Carroll came to know artists such as John Millais and William Holman Hunt, who often stayed at their house, producing or completing many paintings there. Subsequently Carroll was able to photograph these famous men and their families, in Oxford and in London.

Carroll's first recorded visit to see Thomas Combe at the Press was on *6 March 1857*. On *19 June 1862* he went there expressly to show the paintings to his aunt Lucy Lutwidge and older sisters, Frances and Elizabeth, who were all visiting Oxford at the time, staying nearby in Walton Street. On *24 February 1863* he took Alice and Edith, with Mary PRICKETT, to see the pictures, and on the same day they all visited the MUSEUM OF NATURAL HISTORY.

Alice Liddell, aged eight, by Charles Dodgson

The former St Paul's Church, Walton Street

It was at the Press that Carroll met the Pre-Raphaelite sculptor Thomas Woolner, on *16 July 1863*. Carroll had just completed the first of his drawings for 'Under ground', '*a half length of the heroine*', and wanted to seek Thomas Combe's opinion. Woolner happened to be there, beginning work on the bust of Combe which now stands in the ASHMOLEAN Museum. In true Pre-Raphaelite style, Woolner '*condemned the arms, which he says I must draw from the life*'. Carroll returned to see Woolner twice more in Jericho that month, on *17 and 23 July*, and they met again here, along with Woolner's wife and Holman Hunt, on *14 May 1865*.

 ST PAUL'S CHURCH (FREUD'S)
Walton Street, Jericho

www.freud.eu/cafe-bars/

Now a wine-bar called Freud's, St Paul's was constructed in 1835/6 to cater for the growing population of the evolving suburb of Jericho. St Paul's is where Carroll preached his first-ever sermon in Oxford, on *14 May 1865*, to '*the largest congregation I have yet addressed, 300 or 400 I should think*'. Always reluctant to officiate at services, Carroll was no doubt persuaded by Thomas COMBE, who was a churchwarden, or by Alfred Hackman (1811–74), the vicar, who was also well known to Carroll as the CHRIST CHURCH chaplain. Indeed, it was Hackman who first introduced Carroll to William Holman Hunt, on *13 June 1857*. It is thought that the painting of angels on the ceiling is by Hunt. Carroll also preached at St Paul's on *4 & 18 June* and *15 October 1865*. A few years later Combe provided the funds for Jericho's new and larger High Anglican church of St Barnabas, which opened in 1869 specifically to cater for Jericho's ever-increasing population.

Carroll's diaries contain only one record of a visit to Jericho itself, on *10 March 1863*. He, like many, was probably put off by the suburb's unsavoury reputation, but that day was a special one, when 'town' and 'gown' joined as one in celebrating the marriage of the Prince of Wales. Immediately after the girls had planted their commemorative trees by ⑤ the River CHERWELL, Carroll escorted the whole LIDDELL family, including Alice's grandmother, Mrs Lorina Reeve (1794–1879), to Jericho '*to see the ox roasted whole ..., which was not an exciting spectacle*'.

Port Meadow

If you wish to visit the Treacle Well at BINSEY, and/or the riverbank below GODSTOW:

EITHER continue northwards along Walton Street, with its range of shops and places of refreshment, and turn left down Walton Well Road, which passes over the Oxford Canal and railway to the entrance to PORT MEADOW. From there a track leads straight over the Meadow to the Thames path.

OR you might like to wander through the narrow streets of Jericho to cross the Oxford Canal at the footbridge which is near the end of Canal Street. Turn right along the towpath to reach Walton Well Road and Port Meadow; or left back to the city centre. This part of Jericho is the setting for the dramatic finale of Philip Pullman's *Lyra's Oxford*. A partly imaginary Jericho also features in *Northern Lights*, the first book of Pullman's trilogy, where he invokes a time when 'the wharves along the waterfront in Jericho were bright with gleaming harness and loud with the clop of hooves and clamour of bargaining'.

However, if you wish to return to the city centre, retrace your steps (southwards) along Walton Street, turn left into Little Clarendon Street, and right into Wellington Square. Once known as Rats and Mice Hill, this is where Oxford's former workhouse was situated. Walk down St John Street (1825–35) to the junction with Beaumont Street (laid out in 1822; completed in 1833) and turn left.

17 ASHMOLEAN MUSEUM Beaumont Street

www.ashmolean.org   Closed Mondays

The Ashmolean Museum is something of a wonderland in itself, housing a worldwide array of antiquities and works of art in a building which opened in 1845. There is nothing of *specific* relevance to Alice or Lewis Carroll here, but among the important group of Pre-Raphaelite paintings donated by Martha COMBE are those which Carroll saw at their OXFORD UNIVERSITY PRESS home. Of note these include an 1850 portrait of Thomas Combe by John Millais and Thomas Woolner's bust of Combe, mentioned by Carroll in his diary (*17 July 1863*), plus 'Convent Thoughts', a painting by Charles Allston Collins (1828–1873) which was partly inspired by the Combes' garden within the Press at Jericho. In 1861, John RUSKIN encouraged the Museum to recognise the importance of contemporary art alongside Old Masters when he donated an important group of watercolours.

Godstow

The Perch

Alice in Yonderland

Farther afield, on the River Thames upstream and downstream of Oxford.

Distances:
From OUP to BINSEY: approximately 1½ miles
From Binsey to the Treacle Well: approximately ½ mile (plus return)
From Binsey to GODSTOW: approximately ½ mile

➥ A general history of this area (and of Jericho) appears in *A Towpath Walk in Oxford* (see 'Further Reading').

☞ There are regular return boat trips to this part of the river from Folly Bridge (see ⑧ TRILL MILL STREAM), or it can be reached simply by following the Thames Path (approximately 2 miles from Folly Bridge to Binsey village).

PORT MEADOW

Extending from Walton Well Road in the south as far as GODSTOW and Wolvercote to the north, Port Meadow has been common land since at least the time of the Domesday Book (1086). In essence, the appearance of these 350 acres of river floodplain is little changed from how it would have looked in the 1850s and 1860s (or indeed the 850s or 860s!). *1863* was the year of the marriage of Edward the Prince of Wales (see ⑤ CHERWELL), and one of the celebratory events was held on Port Meadow. This was the Great

Note: *Dates in italics* indicate information taken from Lewis Carroll's diaries.

The King's horses and the King's men from
'The Lion and the Unicorn' (*Looking-Glass*)

Treacle Well in Binsey graveyard

Volunteer Review or 'sham fight' as Oxford's weekly newspaper *Jackson's Oxford Journal* described it. It involved 8,000 men from 'some of the finest bodies of cavalry, artillery, and infantry in the country', and the newspaper estimated that 40,000 to 50,000 people watched the spectacle on 24 June. Carroll was among them, likewise the LIDDELL family, perhaps in the grandstand erected especially for the occasion.

The excitement of the event seems likely to have been fresh in his mind the next day, when Carroll escorted the whole Liddell family on a momentous river trip to Nuneham. There is every reason to think that the battle scenes in *Looking-Glass* are a direct result. So too, perhaps, the White King's question to Alice in the chapter called 'The Lion and the Unicorn': 'Did you happen to see any soldiers, my dear, as you came through the wood?' 'Yes, several thousand, I should think.'

Alice was familiar with Port Meadow from another perspective too, recalling in 1932 that a 'great joy was to go out riding with my father … on Port Meadow, or go to Abingdon through Radley, and there were the most lovely rides through Wytham Woods' to the west of Port Meadow.

 BINSEY

www.binseystmargaret.org.uk

In the graveyard of Binsey's church, which lies about half a mile to the north of the village, is St Frideswide's Well. Both the village and St Margaret's Church are on CHRIST CHURCH land, and its vicar from 1857 to 1891 was Carroll's friend and Christ Church colleague Thomas Jones PROUT.

It was Prout who in 1874 restored the well. It had been revered for centuries as the site of a spring miraculously summoned by Oxford's patron saint, Frideswide, early in the eighth century. The reputed healing properties of the water attracted huge numbers of pilgrims, and it is presumably this well to which the Dormouse refers at the 'Mad Tea-Party'. The three sisters at the bottom of the Dormouse's treacle well clearly represent the three Liddells: 'Elsie' (that is, L. C.) is Lorina Charlotte; 'Lacie' is an anagram of Alice; and 'Tillie' is short for Matilda, the pet-name given to Edith.

The self-illustrated front and back cover of 'Under Ground' which Charles Dodgson gave to Alice Liddell on *26 November 1864*. The original is held at the British Library

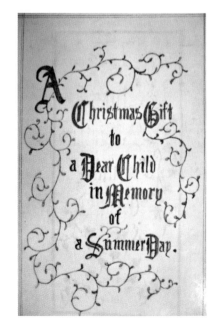

The notion of a treacle well seems at first preposterous, yet is based on an early meaning of the word as a healing liquid or medicine (from the Greek *Thēriakē*, meaning 'antidote'). So there was indeed a treacle well at Binsey, and the fictional Alice – who at first declared: 'There is no such thing!' – was wise eventually to admit that 'I dare say there may be *one*'. It is at the Party that the date of Alice's adventures is revealed as 4 May – Alice Liddell's actual birthday. She is intended to be seven when in Wonderland and seven-and-a-half (as she tells Humpty Dumpty) in *Looking-Glass*, which is set on November 4th.

 If you wish to continue to Godstow from St Margaret's Church, there is no through route: you will have to retrace your steps. However, customers can take a short-cut through The Perch Inn during opening hours.

GODSTOW

It was on the bank of the Thames near the hamlet of Godstow – famous for its 12th-century nunnery and Trout Inn – that the phenomenon of 'Alice' had its birth. Here it was, on Friday *4 July 1862*, that Carroll and his friend Robinson DUCKWORTH stopped for a picnic with the three Liddell sisters. There was nothing especially unusual about this particular fivesome going out on the river together; nor was it out of the ordinary for Carroll to invent stories to keep the girls amused. But the date is enshrined in the history of children's literature as the one when Alice persuaded the versatile mathematics don to write down these impromptu stories for her.

Carroll's immediate diary comment on the day was brief and unremarkable: '*Duckworth and I made an expedition up the river to Godstow with the three Liddells: we had tea on the bank there.*' It is Carroll's later addition which defines the day's supreme significance: '*On which occasion I told them the fairy-tale of "Alice's Adventures Underground", which I undertook to write out for Alice.*' This was the title he selected for the original handwritten manuscript that he presented to Alice – 'in memory of a summer day' – on *26 November 1864*.

Door panel in St Frideswide's Church
carved by Alice's younger sisters:
Rhoda (1859–1949) and Violet (1864–1927) Liddell.

Iffley, seen from above the lock.

Its opening line, no doubt plucked from the reality of that day, was: 'Alice was beginning to get very tired of sitting by her sister on the bank, and of having nothing to do.' It was an expanded version of this original offering that was published the following year as *Alice's Adventures in Wonderland*. The importance of the Godstow river trip is further emphasised by the date Carroll selected for its publication: 4 July.

 ## ST FRIDESWIDE'S CHURCH, OSNEY

www.stfrideswideschurch.org.uk

Back near the city, on the Botley Road a few minutes' walk from the Thames is St Frideswide's Church. Inside there is a carved wooden door showing St Frideswide arriving at BINSEY by boat. It was not, as popularly supposed, carved by Alice Liddell, but was actually done by her sisters, Rhoda and Violet, originally for a church in London. Unfortunately St Frideswide's Church is not normally open except on Sunday mornings and for the occasional public event or community activity.

The Southern River

 From Folly Bridge, the Thames Path passes both IFFLEY and SANDFORD locks, but the farthest relevant destination, Nuneham, some six miles away, is on the opposite bank, and therefore not accessible by foot from the river. However, the Salters' Steamers boat service from Folly Bridge to Abingdon (summer only) provides good views of the house and grounds (www.salterssteamers.co.uk).

IFFLEY

The first river lock downstream from CHRIST CHURCH is at Iffley. This was the destination on the first outing that Alice LIDDELL is known to have taken on the river with Carroll, on 26 May 1862 – although she undoubtedly did accompany him on earlier, unrecorded, trips too. (His diary for the period April 1858 to May 1862 has not survived.) The first

Sandford–on-Thames

Sandford–on-Thames (1878)

boat outing of all, with Lorina and Harry, Alice's older brother, was on *5 June 1856*. That day they went as far as Rose Island, a little downstream from Iffley, and had '*a kind of picnic there, taking biscuits with us, and buying gingerbeer and lemonade*'.

Iffley is the location of a rare indication that Alice's enthusiasm for 'messing about in boats' (to borrow a phrase from *Wind in the Willows*) lasted beyond her childhood years. Queen Victoria's youngest son, Prince Leopold (1853–1884), followed his brother, Albert Edward (the Prince of Wales), to CHRIST CHURCH in 1872, and studied there for three years. In later life, Alice jotted down a recollection that Iffley was where she accidentally hit Leopold with an oar. The two of them were in dread of having to explain the resultant black eye to his mother the Queen (Victoria), since the outing had been unauthorised and unsupervised. But 'I was never ordered to be beheaded,' Alice concluded, in reference, of course, to the Queen of Hearts' favourite expression of 'Off with his/her/their head(s)!'

SANDFORD-ON-THAMES

The episode of 'The Pool of Tears' in *Wonderland* was inspired by an incident at Sandford on a rowing trip to Nuneham on *17 June 1862*. The party that afternoon was an unusually large one. Carroll and the three girls were joined by Robinson DUCKWORTH, apparently for the first time, and two of Carroll's sisters, Elizabeth and Frances. Soon after they had set off upstream for the journey home, it started to pour with rain. They abandoned the boat, and walked to the village of Sandford. Carroll went on ahead with the girls; Duckworth came on behind with Carroll's sisters. Everyone eventually found shelter and dried their clothes in the house of the only person whom Carroll knew well in Sandford, the schoolteacher.

The downpour of rain is commemorated in *Wonderland* by way of Alice's tears, which are so copious that she and several 'curious creatures' are in danger of drowning in the salty pool. Some of these animals are clearly identifiable: the Dodo is Carroll (as an abbreviation of his real name of 'Dodgson'), the Duck is Duckworth, and the Lory and Eaglet represent Lorina and Edith. In *Wonderland* everyone gets dry by running the Caucus-race. In 'Under ground', the original manuscript version of *Wonderland*, Carroll adhered more closely to the reality of the day. The Dodo says, 'I know of a house near here, where we could get the young lady and the rest of the party dried', after which:

> The whole party moved along the river bank…, the Dodo leading the way. After a time the Dodo became impatient, and, leaving the Duck to bring up the rest of the party, moved on at a quicker pace with Alice, the Lory, and the Eaglet, and soon brought them to a little cottage, and there they sat snugly by the fire, wrapped in blankets, until the rest of the party had arrived, and they were all dry again.

Just above Sandford Lock is a large overflow weir, known colloquially as a 'lasher'. It has a mournful past, having claimed the lives of at least five Christ Church scholars, among them in May 1921 Michael Llewellyn Davies, the ward of J. M. Barrie, who composed *Peter Pan* (1904) for Michael and his brothers.

Posthumous portrait (detail) of Charles Dodgson in the Great Hall at Christ Church, by Hubert von Herkomer
(Courtesy of The Governing Body of Christ Church, Oxford. Ref. LP285)